Poor Condition___slightly torn
Marks/Stains _____
GVK Date _____

THE LIBRARY OF FOOD CHAINS AND FOOD WEBS

Food Chains in a
FOREST HABITAT™

ISAAC NADEAU
Photographs by
DWIGHT KUHN

The Rosen Publishing Group's
PowerKids Press
New York

For Jamie and Micah, essential parts of my habitat

Published in 2002 by The Rosen Publishing Group, Inc.
29 East 21st Street, New York, NY 10010

First Edition

Book Design:Emily Muschinske
Project Editor: Emily Raabe

All Photographs © Dwight Kuhn

Nadeau, Isaac.
    Food chains in a forest habitat / Isaac Nadeau.— 1st ed.
        p. cm. — (The library of food chains and food webs)
    ISBN 0-8239-5758-6 (lib. bdg.)
    1. Forest ecology—Juvenile literature. 2. Food chains (Ecology)—Juvenile literature. [1. Food chains (Ecology) 2. Forest ecology.
    3. Ecology.] I. Title. II. Series.
    QH541.5.F6 N34 2002
    577.3'16—dc21

                                                                    00-012323

Manufactured in the United States of America

Contents

What Is a Food Chain?

Every living thing depends on other living things, including people. Guess what that means? You are part of a food chain!

You can find a food chain wherever you find plants, animals, and other living things. A food chain is formed when energy is passed from one plant or animal to another. Plants and animals in the forest use the energy from their food for many things. Energy from food helps plants grow leaves and fruit, and it helps animals swim, fly, and sing. Living things also use the **nutrients** from their food to grow and to keep their bodies strong.

Every creature in the forest has its own way of getting food. Plants get their energy from the sun and their nutrients from the soil. When an animal eats a plant, the plant's energy is passed through the food chain.

When a rabbit eats berries, energy and nutrients are passed from the berries to the rabbit. When a weasel eats the rabbit, energy and nutrients are passed again. The energy and nutrients are passed yet again when an owl eats the weasel. When the owl dies and returns to the soil, another link is made in the food chain.

The Forest Habitat

What is a forest habitat? A habitat is the area where animals or plants live. Most people think of trees when they imagine a forest habitat. Trees, however, are only part of the story.

The forest can be divided into layers. The leafy, top branches of the trees are called the canopy. Below the canopy, smaller trees, shrubs, and other plants form the understory. Plants growing close to the ground make up the herb layer. The forest goes beneath the ground, too. The roots of all of the forest plants are held tightly by soil. Thousands of insects and other animals find food and make their homes in the soil.

Rocks, water, sunlight, and air are also important parts of the forest ecosystem. The term "eco" comes from a Greek word meaning "house." A system is the way things work together as a whole. The word "ecosystem" describes the whole forest and its living and nonliving parts.

A forest is a living community. It is a habitat, or a place where plants and animals have everything they need to live.

Forest Producers

Would you be surprised to learn that you could eat sunlight? Well, that's exactly what plants do. Using special **cells** in their leaves, plants turn sunlight into food energy through a process called **photosynthesis**. Inside the leaf, sunlight is combined with water from the soil and with air to create sugar. Plants use this sugar as food. Plants are called producers. This is because they produce the energy that all of the animals in the forest depend on for food. Plants are the first link in every forest food chain.

The plants have a very important job in the forest. Without them, nothing else would have the energy to live. The next time you eat a salad, remember that you are eating part of the sun!

Right: *Many different trees and shrubs grow in the forest habitat.*

Left: *These are maple tree leaves. Maple trees grow in many eastern forests.*

Left: *Ferns are common in the forest. They grow close to the ground.*

Herbivores in the Forest

Herbivores are helpful to one another, too. When a deer loses its antlers in the fall, many other herbivores feast on them to get calcium, an important nutrient for the growth of bones.

Herbivores are the **vegetarians** of the forest. They are the second link in a food chain. Deer, rabbits, squirrels, and caterpillars are all forest herbivores.

Like the plants, the herbivores play important roles in the forest ecosystem. Some plants depend on herbivores to help them spread their seeds. A squirrel might bury an acorn and then forget about it. That acorn could grow into a new oak tree. Other herbivores, such as the spruce **grouse**, spread the seeds from berries in their **droppings**. Of course, the herbivores are also important to the **carnivores** who eat them!

Clockwise: Moose, red squirrel and luna moth caterpillars are just a few of the many plant eaters that live among the trees.

Who Eats the Herbivores?

Would you know a carnivore if you saw one? Sharp teeth and claws might be your first clues. Carnivores are harder to find in the forest than plants and herbivores because there are fewer of them. Carnivores are the third link in a food chain. Most carnivores eat herbivores, but sometimes carnivores eat other carnivores! For example, an owl might eat a weasel. This food chain would have four links instead of three. There would be a producer, an herbivore, and not just one but two carnivores.

Just like the plants and the herbivores, the carnivores play an important role in the forest. Carnivores help keep the populations of herbivores at a healthy level. Without carnivores to hunt them, there would be too many herbivores for the forest to support. They would eat all of their food supply, and many of them would starve. Some carnivores, like shrews and woodpeckers, feed on insects. These animals are called **insectivores**.

Clockwise from Left: Owls, red foxes and bobcats are forest carnivores.

Forest Predators and Their Prey

Unlike the plant-eating herbivores, most carnivores have to chase their food before they can eat it. Animals that hunt other animals are called predators. The animals that they try to catch are their prey.

Carnivores have **adaptations** to help them catch their prey. Many carnivores, such as foxes, wolves, and weasels, have strong jaws to grip prey tightly and sharp teeth to tear flesh. The sharp **talons** of owls help them in the same way.

Herbivores have their own adaptations to help them avoid being caught by hungry carnivores. Most herbivores have very large ears that make them good at hearing what is around them. They are usually very quiet, and they can move quickly and hide when they sense danger. They must be very **alert** to avoid being eaten! Many herbivores also have **camouflage** to help them blend with the forest. The spots on a fawn or on a chipmunk are examples of camouflage. These spots help the animal to blend with the forest floor.

Owls have tiny fringes like eyelashes on the front of each feather. These fringes break up the air as it passes over the owl's wings. This helps the owl to fly and to hunt in silence.

Eating the Leftovers

White-footed mice have two front teeth that grow throughout their entire lives. This means that a white-footed mouse can eat very hard food, such as seeds and nuts, without wearing away its teeth.

Do you know people who will eat almost anything? There are lots of animals in the forest like this. Animals that eat a wide range of food, including both meat and plants, are called **omnivores**. People are good examples of omnivores. Black bears and white-footed mice are also omnivores. Many omnivores, such as coyotes, will eat whatever they can catch. If they don't catch anything, they'll eat what they find—even dead animals! Omnivores that eat dead animals are also called **scavengers**. Scavengers are important to the forest because they keep the energy and the nutrients in dead animals from going to waste.

Omnivores such as the coyote (left), and the black bear (above) usually don't have trouble finding food because there are so many things that they like to eat.

Decomposers in the Forest

In many forests, the greatest amounts of nutrients and energy are found in the soil. The soil is where you can find the greatest **variety** of living things. Every member of a food chain in the forest eventually falls to the ground and is taken into the soil. Trees die and fall to the forest floor. The bones of porcupines rot into the soil. Twigs from an old robin's nest and the shell of a dead centipede make their way to the soil.

Tiny insects, mushrooms, and earthworms live in the soil. They are called **decomposers**. Decomposers form the final link in a food chain. Decomposers use the energy and nutrients from dead things. The energy gets used up, but the nutrients are returned to the soil. Now the roots of the plants can use these nutrients, along with the energy from the sun, to grow. The food chain in the forest goes full circle!

Right: *This dead tree is rotting into the soil with the help of tiny decomposers. In time, the tree will rot completely into the ground.*

Top Right: *Mushrooms are an example of a decomposer.*

A Web of Life

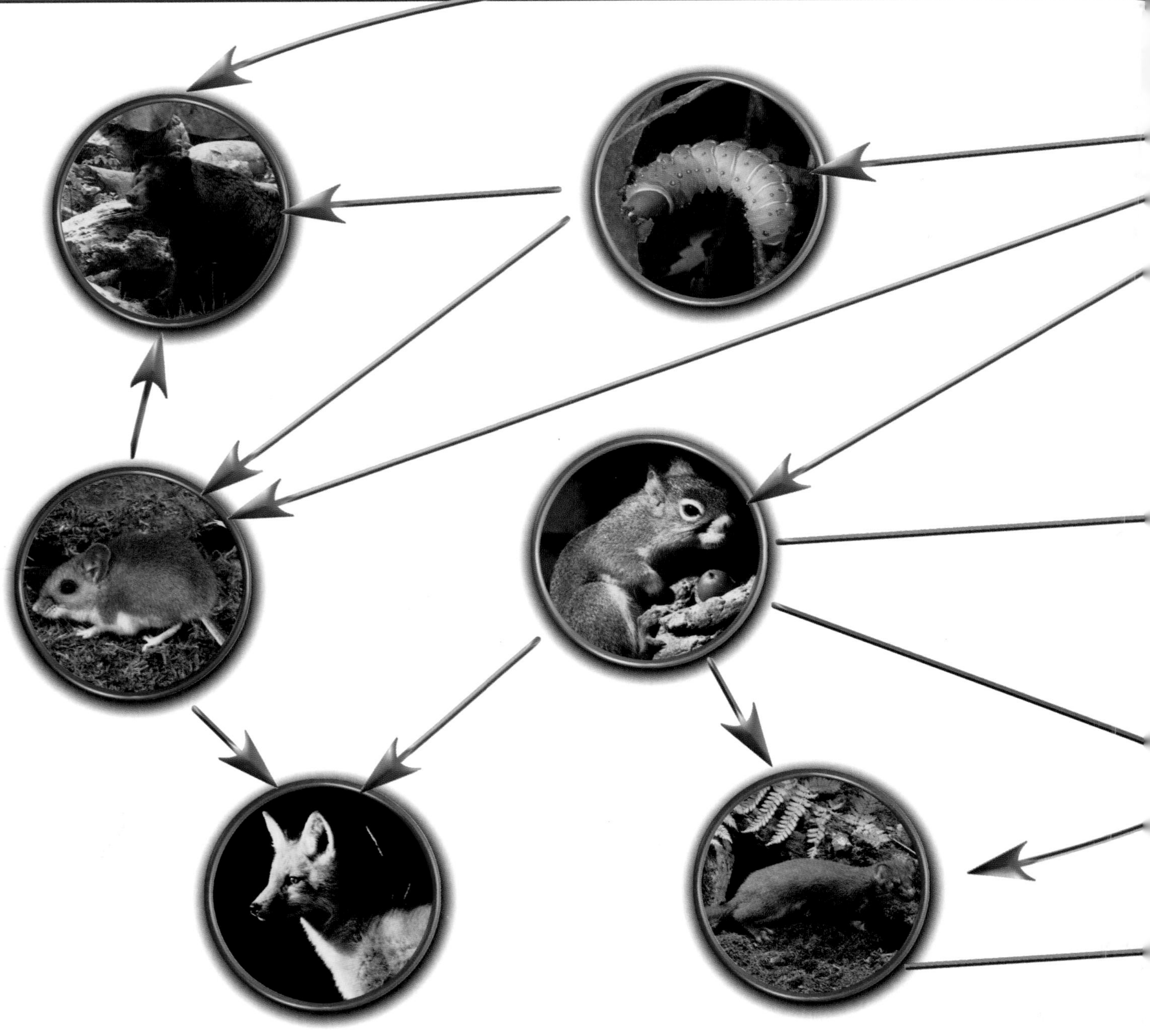

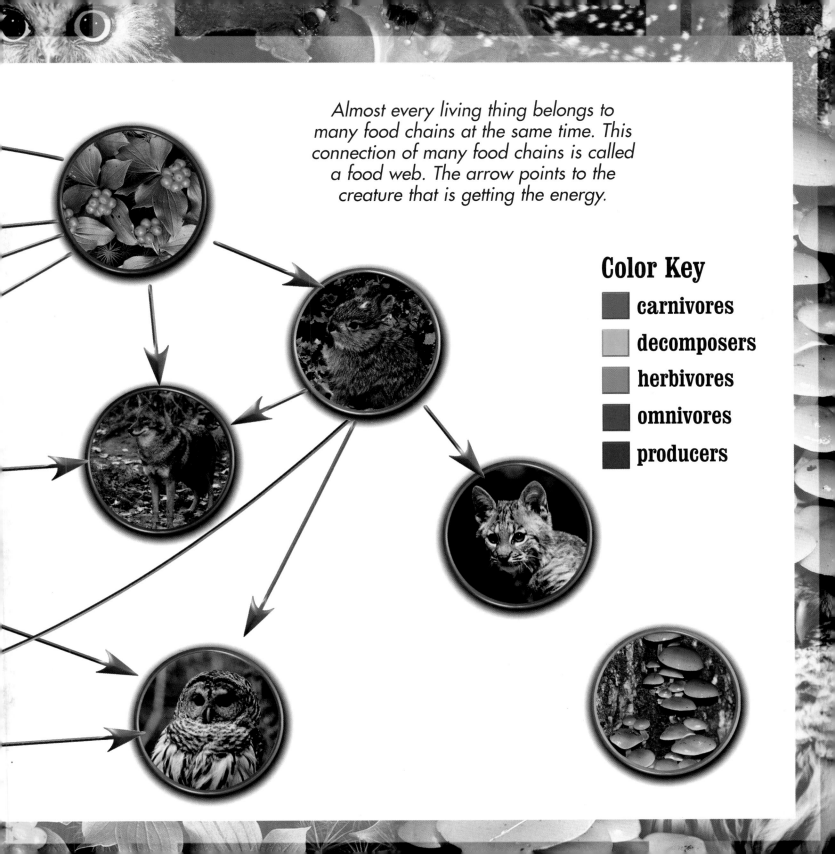

Almost every living thing belongs to many food chains at the same time. This connection of many food chains is called a food web. The arrow points to the creature that is getting the energy.

Color Key

- carnivores
- decomposers
- herbivores
- omnivores
- producers

All Things Are Connected in a Forest

Trees are the lungs of the world. Without them, there would not be oxygen for us to breathe. All of the members of the food web depend on the other members to survive.

Forests have been an important habitat for people all over the world for thousands of years. Like the animals that live there, people depend on the forest for food, materials for building our homes, and space to roam and explore. Just like with the plants and animals, what people do in the forest affects all of the other living things that depend on the forest. For example, by being careful not to waste paper, which is made from trees, we can help to keep the forest a healthy habitat for everyone who lives there. Remember, you are part of the great web of life in the forest habitat!

Glossary

adaptations (a-dap-TAY-shunz) Changes in an animal that help it to survive in its environment.

alert (uh-LERT) Paying attention to what is going on around you.

camouflage (KA-muh-flaj) The color or pattern of an animal's feathers, fur, or skin that helps it blend into its surroundings.

carnivores (KAR-nih-vorz) Animals that eat other animals for food.

cells (SELZ) Tiny units that make up all living things.

decomposers (dee-cum-POH-zerz) Living things that break down the cells of dead plants and animals into simpler parts.

droppings (DRAH-pingz) Animal waste.

grouse (GRAUS) A kind of bird that lives on the ground.

herbivores (ER-bih-vorz) Animals that eat plants for food.

insectivores (in-SEK-teh-vorz) Animals that eat insects for food.

nutrients (NOO-tree-ints) Anything that a living thing needs for its body to live and grow.

omnivores (AHM-nih-vorz) Animals that eat both plants and animals.

photosynthesis (foh-toh-SIN-thuh-sis) The process in which leaves use energy from sunlight, gases from air, and water from soil to make food and release oxygen.

scavengers (SKA-ven-jurz) Animals that eat dead animals they did not kill but found already dead.

talons (TA-lunz) Sharp, curved claws on a bird of prey.

variety (vuh-RY-ih-tee) Many different kinds.

vegetarians (veh-juh-TEHR-ee-uns) People or animals who don't eat meat.

Index

Web Sites

To learn more about food chains in a forest habitat, check out these Web sites:
www.nationalgeographic.com/forest/index.html
www.ran.org/ran/kids_action